**Living Love Forward**

Having a Voice

A Children's Leadership Series

Written by Kim Dawson
Illustrated by Paige Anocibar

Publisher: Tandem Services Press
PO Box 220, Yucaipa, CA 92399
www.tandemservicesink.com

Book Design by Paige Anocibar

ISBN 978-1-954986-23-7

Appreciation to

Inland Leaders Charter School and all our teachers and staff for inspiring and supporting me to write this series.

All my students and their families who taught me to be a better teacher and person.

The 2nd grade, 4th grade, and 5th grade classes at Inland Leaders and Wildwood that gave me GREAT feedback and helped me make this story better!

Pelican Elementary in Oregon for letting us use their school as a model for Lexie's Huckleberry Elementary.

My family and friends who have never wavered in supporting and encouraging my mission to help others.

Paige, my illustrator, for putting up with my "creative" tangents.

Jennifer Crosswhite, my editor and friend, who has been my sounding board and always keeps me positive when I hit the many bumps in the road. (https://www.tandemservicesink.com)

All my readers who have supported me and helped me spread the message that kids can be leaders too.

Sending a ton of love and encouragement to all of you!
We got this!

From the author of the series Living Love Forward:

I wrote this children's leadership series to create an open conversation about the experiences our kids face every day. Being a teacher for over two decades, I have created connections with kids of all ages. I have observed and learned a lot through these interactions and have discovered key skill sets that I think are important for their growth. My purpose in writing these sentimental and caring stories is the hope that they instill life skills and resilience in our children. In turn, this empowers them to become successful and compassionate people, as well as strong leaders. Join Lexie and our children as they navigate this journey of self-discovery.

Please note that this series can be used in conjunction with any Leadership Program focused on survival skills and effective habits for children.

This book specifically focuses on:

- **Finding a voice**
- **Confrontation**
- **Frustration**
- **Lack of social skills**
- **Poor self esteem**
- **Anxiety**

Map of Harlow

Train Station

Church Of Hope

Cemetery

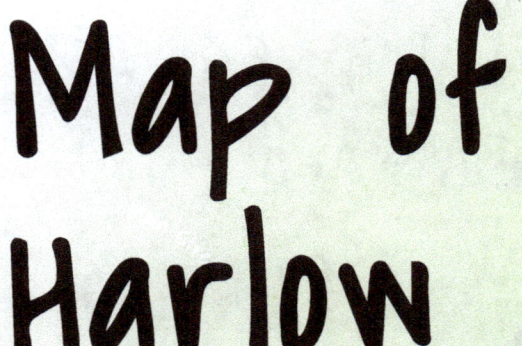

Liberty Library

4th Street

2nd Street

1st Street

Rose Road

Daisy Lane

Main Street

Lexie's House

Bus Stop

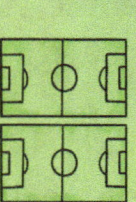

Main Street

Lavendar Lane

Lotus Loop

Jackson Sports Park

Jasmine Avenue

Riverside Park

Rose Road

Huckleberry Elementary

Lavendar Lane

Jasmine Avenue

Annabelle's House

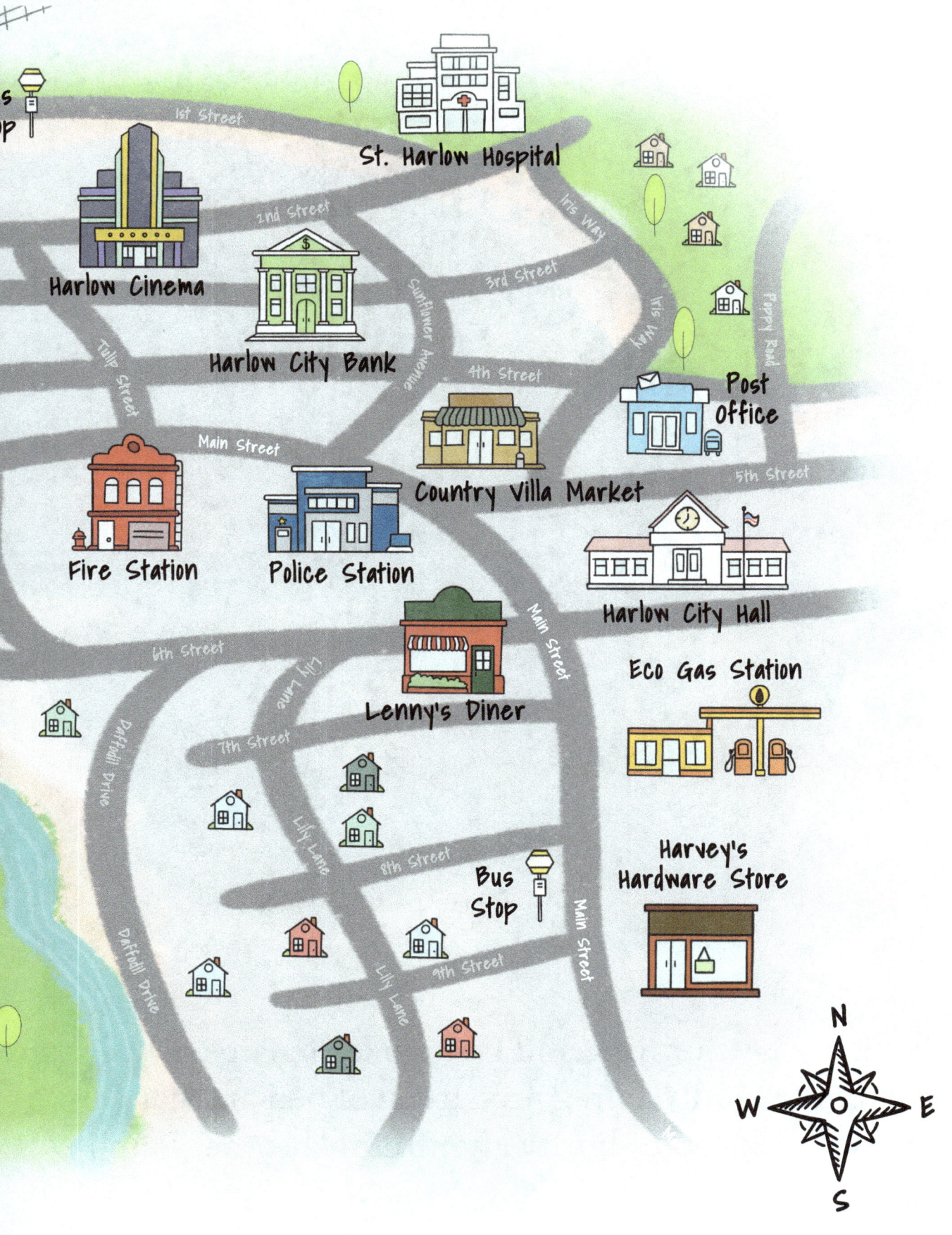

It's Saturday morning and Dad wakes me up early.
I grumble loudly. I drag myself out of bed and get
dressed. We leave shortly after for my brother Sam's
soccer game.

As we head down the street, Dad glances at me over his shoulder with a look of worry on his face. "Lexie, you have been really quiet this morning. Quieter than usual. You ok?"

I just nod my head and continue to look out the window as we drive down Main Street. We need to stop by the Country Villa Market for snacks before going to Sam's game. I notice we are almost at the store as I refocus my attention on the scenes playing outside my window. I see Mrs. Kirkland walking her dog, Scooter, down the street and then we pass the station where the firemen are outside washing the big fire engine. It's a normal day here in Harlow, but I feel off and can't really figure out why.

3

We finally pull into the store parking lot and start to get out of the car. Dad stops and looks back at me when I abruptly shout out, "Dad, why are people so mean?"

"Why do you ask?" Dad questions.

I sigh as I get out and close my car door. Dad comes over to me as I respond quietly, "I know I don't talk all the time, but I feel like people just assume they know what I want. It's that or they cut me off and talk about what they want to talk about."

We start to walk towards the store as I continue to tell him about what happened with Annabelle just yesterday. She had asked me at recess what I wanted to play and I said four-square. She said that basketball would be more fun. Then she dragged me over to the court where some of our friends were already playing.

As Dad leads me into the store I say, "Why did she ask me if she was going to do what she wanted to do anyway? That was really mean."

"Do you think Annabelle was trying to hurt your feelings?" he asks.

I thought a moment. "No, she is my best friend! I think she was just excited to play. She has been trying to get me to sign up for basketball with her. Tryouts are in two weeks," I share.

I still feel upset as we walk towards the produce section to grab the oranges for Sam's snacks. I continue to tell Dad about the other stuff that is bothering me.

I tell him about the time when Mrs. Bryce, my teacher, asked me to answer a question during math.

"I guess I didn't answer fast enough and she moved on and asked Charlie instead," I complain.

As we stand in the checkout line, I tell him about another time when the yard duty, Ms. Lizzy, cut me off when I tried to tell her there were bad words written on the bathroom wall. I told Dad how she had sighed and said that she was right in the middle of something and that I needed to go play.

"I didn't even finish my sentence, Dad!" I sigh with frustration.

As we walk back to our car, Dad says, "Wow… you seem to have a lot on your mind. I can see why you are upset." Then he asks, "Lexie, are they really being mean though and trying to purposely hurt your feelings? Sounds like you need to work on finding your voice."

"What does that mean, to have your own voice?" I ask in confusion.

Dad opens my door and pauses to think. Eventually, he says that having a voice means KNOWING that what you have to say matters. Then you find the courage deep inside to share your thoughts no matter what others might think.

He looks at me and suggests that maybe next time someone cuts me off, I can say, "Whoa!...back up the pony cart... I'm almost done with what I was going to say." Then he suggests making a funny face to keep things lighthearted but still stand my ground.

We leave and start to drive toward Sam's game. Once
we hit Main Street, Dad continues by saying, "We all
get excited or overwhelmed at times just like Annabelle
did. When this happens, we can interrupt and share our
thoughts instead of being a good listener. It still doesn't
make it okay. It is then our job to make sure that we are
heard. We all need to find our own voice so that others
understand what we need and want," he explains.

All weekend I think about what Dad said about how I need to find my voice. When Monday comes around, I decide to see if I can do this. It isn't until lunch time that I get a chance to talk with Annabelle. As I walk to the cafeteria, I see her waving at me from the lunch tables.

Her name is Fluffy and...

I go over and sit down next to her and start to tell her about my weekend. She interrupts and says, "You are not going to believe it...we got a new puppy! Her name is Fluffy and..."

I reach out and put my hand on her arm. She stops talking and looks at me funny. I take a deep breath... and then say, "I would like to share my weekend with you first this time, then we can talk about Fluffy!" Surprisingly, she is okay with this and even ends up apologizing for the times she interrupted me. This makes me feel good.

Dad calls us when we get home from school to tell us he's going to be home late. He's a nurse in the Emergency Room and he helps a lot of people. He does a lot for us too. I decide that Sam and I are going to do a surprise for him tonight. We are going to make him dinner. I call for Sam and we get to work.

When Dad finally gets home he looks exhausted.

He yells to us, "What do you want for dinner?" I run into the living room to tell him about our surprise! He cuts me off mumbling something about the leftover spaghetti in the refrigerator.

I touch his arm to get his attention and he looks down at me. I say, "Dad, I know you are really tired, but remember when we had that conversation about how I needed to find my voice? Well, I have something to share and I think that pony of yours needs to back his cart up." He looks at me with confusion and I start to laugh. Then I lead him by the hand to the kitchen.

When we enter, Sam is there with his hands up yelling, "Surprise!" On the table, there are plates with peanut butter and jelly sandwiches and glasses of orange juice, his favorite.

Dad looks at the dinner table and then at us. He smiles in understanding and whispers in my ear, "I like your voice!"

Author's Advice

* What you think and feel matters.

* People can accidentally hurt your feelings.

* Having a voice does NOT mean being rude or disrespectful. It is simply sharing your thoughts in a kind and honest way.

* Remember that everyone's voice is important, so don't cut off other people's voice either.

* EVERYONE struggles with having a voice. You are not alone...even adults struggle sometimes.

Think and Feel

Can you think of a time when you struggled having a voice? What did you do? If it happened again, would you change anything?

Glossary

abruptly

Definition: sudden and not expected

Part of Speech:

This word is a (noun, adjective, verb, **adverb**).

Evidence of how the word is used in the story.

When Lexie asks "Why are people mean?" She says this abruptly (suddenly).

assume

Definition: to suppose (something) to be true without knowing the actual facts; take for granted.

Part of Speech:

This word is a (noun, adjective, **verb**, adverb).

Evidence of how the word is used in the story.

Lexie is talking to Dad about how people assume (they know without asking) what she wants.

Glossary

frustration

Definition: an angry or impatient feeling caused by not being able to do something

Part of Speech:

This word is a (**noun**, adjective, verb, adverb).

Evidence of how the word is used in the story.

Lexie feels frustrated (angry) when she is talking to Dad about how people are being mean to her.

refocus

Definition: to look at something again

Part of Speech:

This word is a (noun, adjective, **verb**, adverb).

Evidence of how the word is used in the story.

Lexie is upset and is looking out the window when her dad asks her a question. After she answers, she looks out the window and refocuses (to look at something again) her attention outside.

Glossary

Whoa!...back up the pony cart

Definition: slow down, stop, and regroup

Language Usage:

"Whoa" is an interjection
(an interjection is a word or expression that shows strong feeling; exclamation. Examples: "Oh no!" and "Oops!")

"Whoa!...back up the pony cart" is an idiom
(An idiom is a phrase that means something different than the literal words being used. Examples: "It is raining cats and dogs" means it is raining very hard and "Go break a leg!" means go try your hardest)

Evidence of how it is used in the story.

Dad says to Lexie that when she is interrupted she can say, "Whoa!..back up the pony cart." (slow down, stop, and regroup) and then finish telling her story.

yard duty

Definition: An adult that watches kids at recess or break to make sure everyone stays safe.

Part of Speech:

This word is a (**noun**, adjective, verb, adverb).

Evidence of how the word is used in the story.

Lexie talks to Dad about the yard duty (adult that watches kids at recess) who doesn't listen to her.

About the Author: Kim Dawson

I am a single mom of two wonderful kids. I have been teaching for a number of decades and love spending time with my students. I have been writing since I was a child. It has always been a way for me to express myself when I am struggling. I strongly believe that we do not give our kids the credit they deserve. They have a lot to teach us if we just listen.

About the Illustrator: Paige Anocibar

Art is my passion. Every day I am thankful to have a career that empowers me to express myself through creativity. Drawing has been a part of my life since I was a small child. Coloring and painting were my favorite part of going to school. Back then, just like now, I was eager for the next art project. I knew that expressing myself through art is all I have ever wanted to do with my life, and illustrating this book has helped me achieve a part of that dream.

If you enjoyed this story, see other books in this Children's Leadership series, Living Love Forward.

2023 Books

February   May   September   November

2024 Books

February   May   September   November